TOTNES

TOTNES

Totnes Museum Society

Totnes Museum

First published in Great Britain by The Mint Press, 2003

© Jill Drysdale, Todd Gray, Walter King, and Bob Mann in respect to their chapters 2003

The rights of Jill Drysdale, Todd Gray, Walter King, and Bob Mann to be identified as authors of this work has been asserted by them in accordance with the Copyright, Designs & Patents Act 1988.

All rights reserved. No part of this publication may be reproduced in any form or by any means without the prior permission of the copyright holders

Hardback edition ISBN 1-903356-34-2
Softback edition ISBN 1-903356-35-0

Cataloguing in Publication Data
CIP record for this title is available from the British Library

The Mint Press
18 The Mint
Exeter, Devon
England EX4 3BL

Typeset in Frutiger by TOPICS – The Creative Partnership, Exeter
Cover design by Delphine Jones

Printed and bound in Great Britain
by Short Run Press Ltd, Exeter

Contents

Foreword *The Duke of Somerset*	vii
Introduction *Todd Gray*	ix
General Views *Bob Mann*	1
The River *Bob Mann*	13
Bridgetown *Bob Mann*	33
The Bridge *Walter King*	38
Buildings *Walter King*	47
St Mary's Church *Jill Drysdale*	78
The Castle *Jill Drysdale*	88
Country Houses *Todd Gray*	94
Bibliography and Illustration Sources	100

Acknowledgements

The Totnes Museum Society would like to thank Barry Weekes of the Totnes Image Bank, Katherine Dunhill of the Westcountry Studies Library, Sue Laithwaite of the Devon Record Office and Sue King, Co-ordinator of the Totnes Museum Study Centre for their assistance with the book. We would also like to thank Mr W. G. Bennett MBE, Mr Eric Dancer CBE, Judy Westacott, Mayor of Totnes, Mrs J. S. Drysdale, Mr Francis Naylor and the Mitchell Trust for their generous support which has helped to make this book possible. The illustrations come from the collection of the Totnes Museum, the Devon Record Office and Westcountry Studies Library who have graciously granted permission to publish them.

Foreword

Totnes has captivated visitors and its inhabitants for generations. This collection of unknown and unusual images offers rare delights illustrating how the town has changed during the last two hundred years. There are strange perspectives, lost buildings, views of familiar places in unfamiliar ways. Each and every image reinforces an existing love of Totnes by those who have already been seduced by its charms and will make the town known to countless more. This book will provide many hours of enjoyment.

I commend the Totnes Museum Society in making these images available to the wider public and am confident that they will be widely cherished.

I warmly recommend this book,

The Duke of Somerset

Introduction

This book is a collection of printed and original views of Totnes created by a number of artists from the eighteenth to twentieth centuries. Most of the drawings have never been previously published and many of the prints are no longer available. The images are drawn from collections at the Totnes Museum, Devon Record Office and Westcountry Studies Library. There are two main series of original illustrations. The first is a set of twelve paintings by Robert H. Froude who was born in 1771 and died in 1849. These were made between 1793 and 1841. Froude knew Totnes well: he became rector of Dartington in 1799 and afterwards Archdeacon of Totnes. He is as well known for three sons: Richard Hurrell was a divine and connected with the Tractarians, James Anthony became an historian and man of letters, and William was an engineer and naval architect. The second is a series of twelve pencil sketches by N. W. Deckamant. He drew these while on a short visit to Totnes on the 6th and 21st of August 1856. The drawings form part of his *Illustrations of the Antiquities of the Counties of Devon, Dorset and Cornwall*. The styles of each man are very different and yet each drawing is very informative.

The artists who came to Totnes produced work which showed the town in a positive way and mostly concentrated on picturesque aspects of it. Some are particularly unreliable as historical records: J. M. W. Turner's view of the town, for instance, is highly stylised. In contrast, Mr Deckamant seems to have been more interested in accurately drawing the buildings and not in depicting atmosphere. Some older photographs have been included in this collection in order to contrast the buildings with their depiction by other artists. They show some of the inaccuracies of the prints and drawings particularly in relation to perspective. They also show how certain scenes were popular. General views, images of the river and street scenes, particularly Fore Street, dominate but there are many drawings of individual buildings.

The history of Totnes can be seen through the depicted buildings. The wealth from the cloth trade made it possible to erect the imposing sixteenth and seventeenth-century timber-heavy slate-hung houses favoured by merchants. They crowd Fore and High Streets and give an impression

Undated wood engraving by A. Barraud entitled 'Totnes, from the Dart'.

of grand solidity. In the eighteenth-century the cloth industry declined in Totnes as it did in the rest of Devon. The town dwindled in importance but neighbouring places increased in size and influence through other factors. Newton Abbot greatly benefited from the arrival of the railway in the 1840s and Torquay and Teignmouth were redeveloped as Gentry resorts. Totnes became a sleepy market town and its lack of great wealth in the nineteenth and early twentieth centuries helped to preserve many of its buildings. This urban decline later contributed to Totnes' appeal in the twentieth-century to visitors who viewed it as picturesque, not a description now easily assumed by its largely Victorian neighbour Newton Abbot. Many of the buildings for which Totnes is known can be seen through the drawings and engravings in this collection and the differences between now and then can be intriguing.

This book will not greatly change our understanding of the history of Totnes. It has been more than a generation since the last comprehensive research on the town's history was published and since that time much has been learned about individual aspects of Totnes but there are many documents in the county record office and in the national archives which need to be read and examined. At best this collection is a visual history of Totnes, a means by which to glimpse the past and attempt to understand more from it. This is not to trivialise the images. They are important because they make us think differently about places we know and imagine buildings which have long vanished. But until now these images were unique and vulnerable to destruction. Their publication helps to secure their survival for future generations. Just as importantly, they are now accessible to the public; this collection makes each image available on a scale unthinkable to their creators.

Todd Gray

Three early photographs of the top of High Street.

INTRODUCTION

General views

The most popular view of Totnes has always been from the heights to the south east, from Totnes Down Hill, Sharpham Drive or the fields between them. From here, the town's position at the tidal head of the Dart estuary, sloping gently towards the river with Dartmoor in the distance, is best appreciated and most coherently presented. The prospect of the town from the opposite side, from Hamstead and the Newton Abbot road, was equally good for presenting the whole town in its setting.

1. Lithograph by and after William Spreat, c.1850, entitled 'Totnes, from Totnes Down'. Early nineteenth-century Totnes was a comfortable middle class community dominated by lawyers, bankers and service officers. It was well aware of its historical and mythological significance – Brutus, legendary founder of Britain, who was supposed to have landed here in 1170 B.C., appeared in every parade and celebration. The town even displayed a self-conscious 'artiness' very familiar today: in an article for the Monthly Magazine in 1808 Milford Windeatt provided an extravagant encomium on Totnes, praising its beauty and wholesome atmosphere, and extolling the enlightenment and creativity induced in its inhabitants by the loveliness of their surroundings. In the following issue a Totnesian resident in London tartly asked where he could find the 'works of erudition, genius and philosophy' engendered by his hometown. Views of Totnes from the hills emphasised the romantic setting and rich hinterland.

TOTNES

2. Lithograph by William Spreat, c.1850, entitled 'Totnes, from Breakheart Field near Sharpham Lodge'. The image of Totnes as a place of genteel cultivation is clearly presented here, with little sign of any work being done. The tree-lined avenue of New Walk leading from The Plains to St Peter's Quay, the transformation of the island into a pleasure park and the old houses climbing the hill towards the castle all speak of a fashionable taste for the picturesque.

GENERAL VIEWS

3. Undated lithograph. From the early 1800s Romantic travellers in search of the beautiful and sublime would be rowed up and down the river in order to inspect the seats and gardens of Sharpham, Greenway and Sandridge. The first regular paddle steamer service began in 1837, after the Duke of Somerset instigated regular dredging, but a trial was made in the summer of 1836 to test the viability of the idea. A young Totnes saddler called John Webber Chaster clearly approved, confiding to his diary that the steamer 'already appears to supersede the passage boats, for surely one would rather be walking the deck of a steamer than be cooped up with tinkers, chimney sweeps and organ grinders in a working tub.'

4–5. *Two aquatint/etchings by and after F. C. Lewis, 1820. Early nineteenth-century Totnes consisted of little more than the original hilltop Saxon walled town, with the long street stretching down to the river, although draining of the surrounding marshes had been going on gradually since the thirteenth century.*

GENERAL VIEWS

TOTNES

6. Steel line engraving by H. Wallis after G. B. Campion, c.1832, of Totnes from Sharpham Drive. Parts of the wall still survive, though there were probably fewer spacious Georgian houses, reminiscent of Bath, than the artist suggests. Likewise, the Dartmoor hills in the distance seem slightly exaggerated.

GENERAL VIEWS

7. Steel line engraving after George Townsend, c.1855. The view of Totnes from the Littlehempston direction gives a comprehensive idea of the extent of the town. Brunel's South Devon Railway arrived in 1847 and was intended to be worked by the Atmospheric method, though in fact this was abandoned before the trains began running. The tower of the pumping station can be seen to the far right.

TOTNES

8. Lithograph by and after William Spreat, c.1850, entitled 'Totnes, from Hamstead'. Another prospect from the north shows how Bridgetown, incorporated into the borough after the 1832 Reform Act, had become a genteel suburb on the opposite side of the Dart.

GENERAL VIEWS

9. Lithograph by and after George Rowe, c.1826, entitled 'Totness, Devon'. A peaceful view of the town from the Littlehempston side shows Totnes as a pastoral idyll.

TOTNES

10. Coloured wash by R. H. Froude entitled 'approach to Totnes, No. 1, 1827'. Archdeacon Froude's atmospheric view of the town from the north before the building of the railway emphasises the compact, self-contained nature of early nineteenth-century Totnes.

GENERAL VIEWS

11. An undated view of Totnes from Bridgetown, in which the castle, church tower and Dartington Hall in the distance, are greatly exaggerated for picturesque effect.

TOTNES

12. It is not easy to work out the viewpoint of this busy impression of the town, but it must be from near Steamer Quay. The Island, now Vire Island, was created out of several small lumps and eyots in the river and joined up to Fowler's 1828 bridge.

The River

Totnes owes its existence to the river Dart, which has always been a highway of trade and communication. Like many Devon rivers it gradually became silted up during the sixteenth and seventeenth centuries, and this was blamed on the activities of the Dartmoor tinners. Early in the nineteenth century the 11th Duke of Somerset, lord of Bridgetown and Berry Pomeroy, and the most dominant local landowner, began embanking and dredging which saved Totnes as a port. The river also became a favourite way of arriving or departing from the town.

13. Steel line engraving after George Townsend, 1861. Looking towards Totnes from the hills beyond the Longmarsh, a mile-long stretch on the Bridgetown bank created in the 1830s by the Duke of Somerset and a favourite walk ever since. The small sailboat in the foreground is typical of those used for transporting goods up and down.

14. Lithograph by and after O. Angel, c.1840, entitled 'Totnes from the Dart'. The river is as placid as a millpond in this view from the vicinity of World's End. Parts of the wall on the left still survive.

THE RIVER

15. Line engraving entitled 'View of the river Dart, looking towards Totness', by William LePetit after Thomas Allom, 1829–32.

16. Steel line engraving by T. Heawood after E. M. Wimperis, c.1830, entitled 'On the Dart, near Totnes'. A gentle pastoral view looking down from near the St Peters Quay area, showing what is now Baltic Wharf.

THE RIVER

17. Line engraving after W. H. J. B., 1911. The right bank shows the present site of the Rowing Club and car park, while on the left is Baltic Wharf.

TOTNES

18. Mezzotint by C. Turner after J. M. W. Turner, 1825. Turner's famous view of Totnes owes nothing to topographical accuracy and everything to his unique inner vision. Trying to locate his viewpoint is as pointless as enumerating his departures from reality, but it must have been somewhere on the Longmarsh.

19. Undated line drawing. No one journeying up the Dart will ever forget the first appearance of the town, dominated by the red sandstone tower of St Mary's. The impact of the initial sight of the tower is well captured here.

TOTNES

20. Undated line drawing by E. W. Charlton. The luxuriance of growth in this view of the Longmarsh is almost tropical.

THE RIVER

21. Copper line engraving by J. Walker after T. Girton, 1801. A shorthand impression of Totnes from the river needs only the castle and church tower to be instantly recognisable. This view is from just beyond Steamer Quay. The spelling 'Totness' enjoyed a brief vogue in the late eighteenth and early nineteenth centuries.

22. First of several drawings by R. H. Froude made on 16 July 1835. Archdeacon Froude shows the town as approached from the river, just before what is now Steamer Quay.

THE RIVER

23. Coloured wash by R. H. Froude, 24 May 1841. Looking towards the bridge from the Steamer Quay area, with the island (now Vire Island) on the left.

TOTNES

24. Coloured wash by R. H. Froude, 24 May 1841. Looking downstream from St Peter's Quay.

25. Coloured wash by R. H. Froude, 24 May 1841. From St Peter's Quay, showing the reclaimed town marsh and the mill tail, with the island on the right. Few areas of Totnes have been completely transformed as here: originally tidal marsh separating Totnes from St Peters Quay in the manor of Little Totnes, it was drained in the late eighteenth century and became the pleasure ground of New Walk. It was then a busy industrial quay, and is now covered with housing.

TOTNES

26. Lithograph by W. Spreat after C. F. Williams, c.1845. The tree-lined New Walk, the end of the island and a typically picturesque jumble of riverside buildings create an atmospheric mid nineteenth-century prospect.

27. Soft-ground etching by Samuel Prout, 1811. No activity on the Bridgetown side, but evidence that Totnes is still active as a port on the opposite bank, between St Peter's Quay and Baltic Wharf.

28. Coloured wash by R. H. Froude, 17 April 1827, entitled 'Tucking Mills, Totnes'. From the middle ages onwards, a number of tidal mills stood on the north side of the bridge, many of them used for 'tucking' or fulling cloth.

THE RIVER

29. Coloured wash by R. H. Froude, 11 April 1827 entitled 'Totnes Mills'.

30. Anonymous steel line engraving, 1865. New Walk from the Totnes end, shows the atmospheric Taunton Monument at the far end, a folly-like representation of the town coat of arms or 'Castle and Keys', named for William Doidge Taunton, mayor in 1824. The monument survived until the 1950s.

31. Photograph by A. W. Searley entitled 'Artificial Ruin on Totnes Quay', 1910.

32. Drawing entitled 'Totnes Weir' by R. H. Froude, 1827. The first weir on the Dart at Totnes was built in the late sixteenth century, a little downstream of the present one. It caused flooding on the Littlehempston bank, which led to a long series of troubles and lawsuits for the town. Eventually, in the early eighteenth century, the problem seems to have been solved by moving the channel of the river to the west, and building a new weir.

33. Engraving entitled 'Fish house on the Dart, near Totnes' by Fuller, 1849. The fish house stood next to the weir. It was washed away by floods in 1894. The height of the weir, and the hills on the Littlehempston side, seem slightly exaggerated.

Bridgetown

Bridgetown originated in the thirteenth century when the Pomeroys of Berry Pomeroy planted a borough on their side of the Dart, hoping to gain a share of the river trade. A three-day fair was granted in 1267, and by 1293 the borough had fifty-five burgesses. A pottery existed here, and much of the crude, orange-red medieval pottery found in and around Totnes was made in Bridgetown. The borough never achieved corporate independence from the manor and parish of Berry Pomeroy, and became part of Totnes in 1832. The community retained a certain separateness however, as tolls had to be paid for crossing the bridge, and throughout the nineteenth century it had many pubs and shops between the bridge and the Newton Abbot road. The Victorian Dukes of Somerset built several fine houses and rows of model workmen's cottages, and by the end of the century many of the wealthier traders and professional men of Totnes lived here. In the twentieth century new estates covered the hills and fields of Bridgetown, and it still retains a sense of its own identity.

34. Anonymous steel line engraving, after Fuller. New, genteel nineteenth-century Bridgetown rises across the river, seen from the island.

35. This view by Edna Arthur of the older part of Bridgetown shows the interesting range of buildings, from the seventeenth to the nineteenth centuries, to be seen there. St John's church was built in the 1830s and designed to echo St Mary's in Totnes. The Seymour Hotel is now flats.

BRIDGETOWN

36. Pencil drawing by N. W. Deckamant, 1856, of Bridgetown.

TOTNES

37. Coloured wash by R. H. Froude, 23 April 1827, entitled 'From west end of Bridgetown, entrance on W. Bridge'. The view from Bridgetown as the new bridge designed by Charles Fowler nears completion.

BRIDGETOWN

38. Coloured wash by R. H. Froude, 9 October 1839, entitled 'From the bridge at Totnes'. Nineteenth-century warehouses line the Bridgetown bank and the island is on the right in this rather elongated view from the new bridge.

The Bridge

Totnes stands at the lowest practical fording point on the Dart, close to the reach of high tide. This may well be the original reason for its existence. Rivers presented barriers to an invading army, enforcing long detours to the point where at last a crossing could be risked. Such a location became strategically important and required defending. The conquering Romans, landing on the south coast, were unable to cross the Thames until they reached the site of the present day London Bridge, where they founded Londinium. Similar considerations gave rise to Gloucester on the Severn and Exeter on the Exe, in each case securing the crossings nearest the sea.

The same logic applied to defending armies. Eight centuries later, when subjected to repeated Viking raids, the Saxons under Alfred built fortified settlements in Devon at Exeter, Pilton, Lydford and Halwell. But within a short time, it seems that those at Pilton and Halwell were abandoned, perhaps with Roman logic in favour of new riverside locations at the lowest safe crossing points. In the case of Pilton, it was to the Taw at Barnstaple, and in the case of Halwell, to the Dart: at Totnes.

It seems inevitable that soon after the foundation of Totnes around 900 A.D., attempts would be made to bridge the crossing, and that a succession of flimsy wooden structures served for a while before being swept away in the winter floods. But tradition has it that the first bridge across the Dart at Totnes was built in the reign of King John. The earliest record is of about 1250, when the bridge chapel was founded at its western end. Evidence is compelling that it was made of wood: during the 1400s it was in constant need of repair, and in particular, in 1451, the wardens of the bridge were ordered to place 'gravyll' upon its 'plankys'. The Mayor's Court ordered further extensive repairs in 1475–6.

A more permanent structure was urgently needed.

39. Line drawing by Edna Fry. Approaching Totnes from the bridge, showing the toll house on the right and the warehouses of Town Quay on the left.

40. Lithograph by William Spreat entitled 'Totnes from the bridge', no date given. A lively mid-nineteenth century impression of the main street from the bridge. Many buildings and features are unchanged. The toll gates were publicly burned in 1881.

TOTNES

41. Coloured wash by R. H. Froude entitled 'bridge, Totnes', 1793. In 1540 when John Leland had completed his Itinerary, he had noted that 'Totnes bridge has 7 archis', clearly a description of the first stone bridge, presumably built between 1451 and 1540, and seen here looking downstream with the quay buildings to the right. This sketch was made by the young Robert Hurrell Froude (1771–1859), later rector of Dartington and Archdeacon of Totnes.

THE BRIDGE

42–3. Two images with some differences. Here is a view from the eastern bank, in front of the Somerset (later Seymour) Arms. To appreciate what this old bridge was like, visit Staverton Bridge. The two were built at about the same time and were practically identical, in the shape and number of arches, the width (ten feet), and the triangular pedestrian refuges. The poplar behind is a reminder that eighteenth century topographical views of Totnes (see, for example the copy in the museum) show that the countryside around was strangely dominated by hundreds of these slender trees.

44. This drawing of unknown origin from the same viewpoint appears to be broadly topographically accurate. Note the glimpse of the gabled Norris's Almshouses on the corner of Fore Street and the Plains.

THE BRIDGE

45. View by S. Alken after Yorke, 1804. By the 1820s the old bridge, although still in good condition, was too narrow to bear the increasing traffic, as Bridgetown was beginning to grow in size and population.

It is at length determined to widen and repair the bridge across the Dart at Totnes forthwith. In the late flood, the water reached within a few feet of the highest part of this ancient bridge, and it remained firm and uninjured. It is thought to be out of the power of modern architecture, to erect a more substantial structure, therefore the intention of taking it down is abandoned.
Exeter Flying Post, 10 April 1823

Notwithstanding this bizarre claim, after some debate it was decided to replace the old bridge with a new one. This downstream view (dated 1804) had been completely transformed by 1831 as both the old bridge and Bridge House (seen here to the left of the print) had been demolished, the latter to make way for Seymour Terrace, part of the Duke of Somerset's scheme for the development of Bridgetown.

TOTNES

46. Another sketch by R. H. Froude, 1827, and entitled 'Totnes Bridge as it was when in hand for –'. It shows the new bridge being constructed alongside the old.

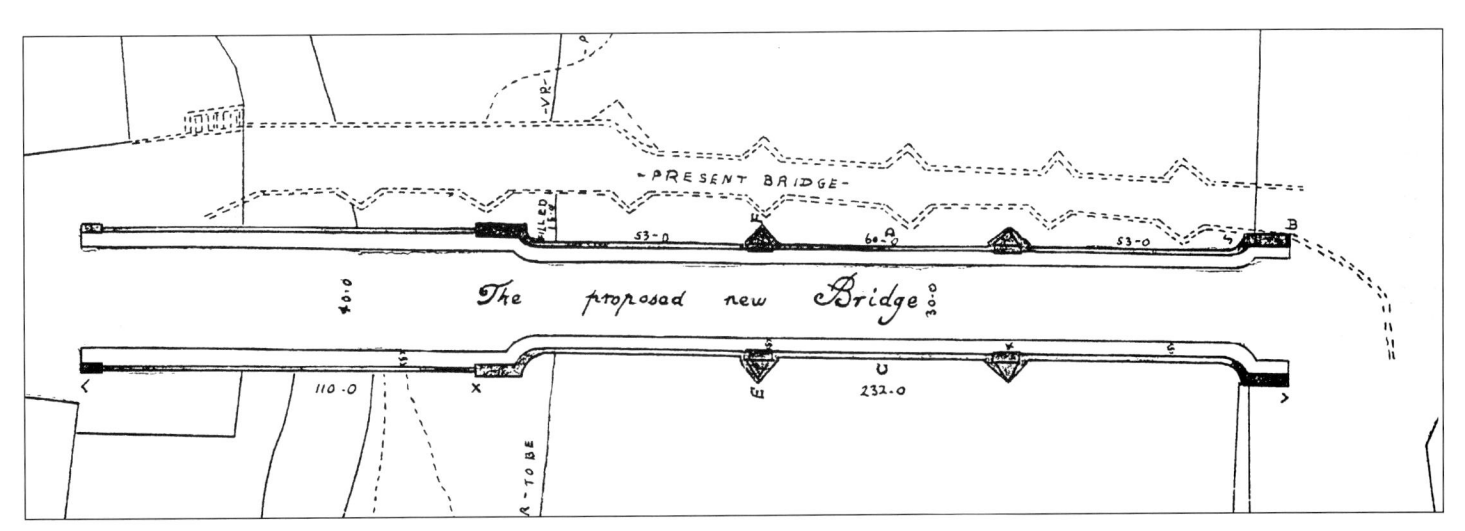

47–8. Plan, elevation and map of the new bridge. Thus the direct alignment of Fore Street with the bridge was to be lost. Traces of the stone bridge can still be seen on both banks at low tides.

A number of labourers are now employed in clearing the site for the new bridge across the Dart, Totnes. It is to be built a little below the old bridge, and a house or two at the lower end of the town will be taken down.

Exeter Flying Post, 2 February 1826

We omitted to notice in our last week's paper, that the new bridge over the Dart at Totnes had been opened to the public. The ceremony took place last week when there was numerous assemblage of the Commissioners on the occasion who proceeded in a body to inspect the works, and having passed over the old bridge for the last time, the workmen immediately closed up the barriers: the party then returned over the new bridge and were greeted by the cheers of an immense concourse of persons. At the same moment guns were fired, and a band of music struck up the national anthem "God Save the King". The day being remarkably fine, a vast influx of visitors had been attracted from the surrounding neighbourhood, who all seemed gratified in joining to celebrate the completion of an interesting work, the design and execution of which reflect great credit on all the parties concerned. The workmen were regaled with a plentiful supper at the Somerset Arms, and the Commissioners, with a large party of Gentlemen, sat down to an excellent supper at the Seven Stars.

Exeter Flying Post, 10 April 1828

49. Steel line engraving by W. Deeble after T. M. Baynes, 1829. The new bridge was designed by Charles Fowler, a founder of the Institute of British Architects, whose next main work was to be Covent Garden Market in London.

Buildings

Totnes is one of the most rewarding small towns in England, appealing in the visual variety of the small buildings close-packed within the framework of its medieval street plan, intriguing in the exceptional quantity of wealthy merchants' houses surviving from the sixteenth and seventeenth centuries.

Bridget Cherry and Nikolaus Pevsner, *The Buildings of England: Devon*

These buildings date from the time of greatest prosperity in Totnes, when many of the houses along High Street and Fore Street were rebuilt. Sixty-six existing houses have been shown to be pre-1700. Their survival (apart, in some instances, from a fashionable face-lift in the Georgian style or the locally popular slate-hanging) is due to the subsequent decline in the fortunes of Totnes and its merchants. In compiling this selection, we have been constrained by the availability of old prints and paintings, and so many outstanding buildings are un-represented, whereas some lesser (though still interesting) scenes gain entry.

51. *A view looking up Fore Street on the north side of the bridge.*

Mr Thos L. Wildes requests Mrs Cornish to accept a sketch of the Almshouse as it appeared on the 2nd April 1830. It may perhaps be sufficient to preserve the remembrance of an old neighbour, now no more. Totnes, April 20 1830.
A replacement was then erected at the Grove (in its turn demolished around 1969–70) recycling some materials including the stone window frames. A stone tablet from the original building is now in the museum courtyard and bears the inscription dated 1600:

Remember the Poore
God will remember thee.

On 15th April 1836, the corporation of Totnes sold the entire Norris's Almshouses site for £120 to a local carpenter Henry Webber, and he built on it an elegant row of four town houses, since ruined by piecemeal and unsympathetic alterations (see page 48). Number 3 bears a plaque declaring that William Wills, early explorer of Australia was born there, but he was already two years old when it was built and when his family took possession, they lived next door.

50. Pencil sketch by Thomas L. Wildes, 20 April 1830. Norris's Almshouses originally consisted of just a two-storey building containing two rooms at the junction of Fore Street and the Plains. They were erected in 1601 and maintained by means of a legacy from wealthy resident John Norris. The almshouses were later extended southwards down the Plains to create the ten-room structure shown in this view. The activity on the left suggests that the roof is being repaired, but a faint inscription on the back of this pencil sketch tells us that the building was in the process of being dismantled.

BUILDINGS

52. Coloured wash by R. H. Froude, c.1820, entitled 'Mill Lane, Totnes'. The earliest mills were tidal. Twice a day the low land where the industrial estate now stands would flood, and the ebb tide was used to power waterwheels. Sixteenth-century land reclamation robbed the tidal mill of its motive power, and so the weir was built upstream, together with a leat to provide a more conventional power source. The weir in its turn caused periodical flooding, and lawsuits which brought financial ruin on the town, but that is another story. In 1888 there was an extensive water storage lake and central island, with twin sluices and watercourses powering a wheel on both sides of the building, each of which would have driven a mill and lifting hoist. This is a view from what is now the recently pedestrianised Mill Lane looking towards Fore Street. The Seven Stars is at the far left, and across Fore Street at the end of the lane is part of the north end of the Norris Almshouses.

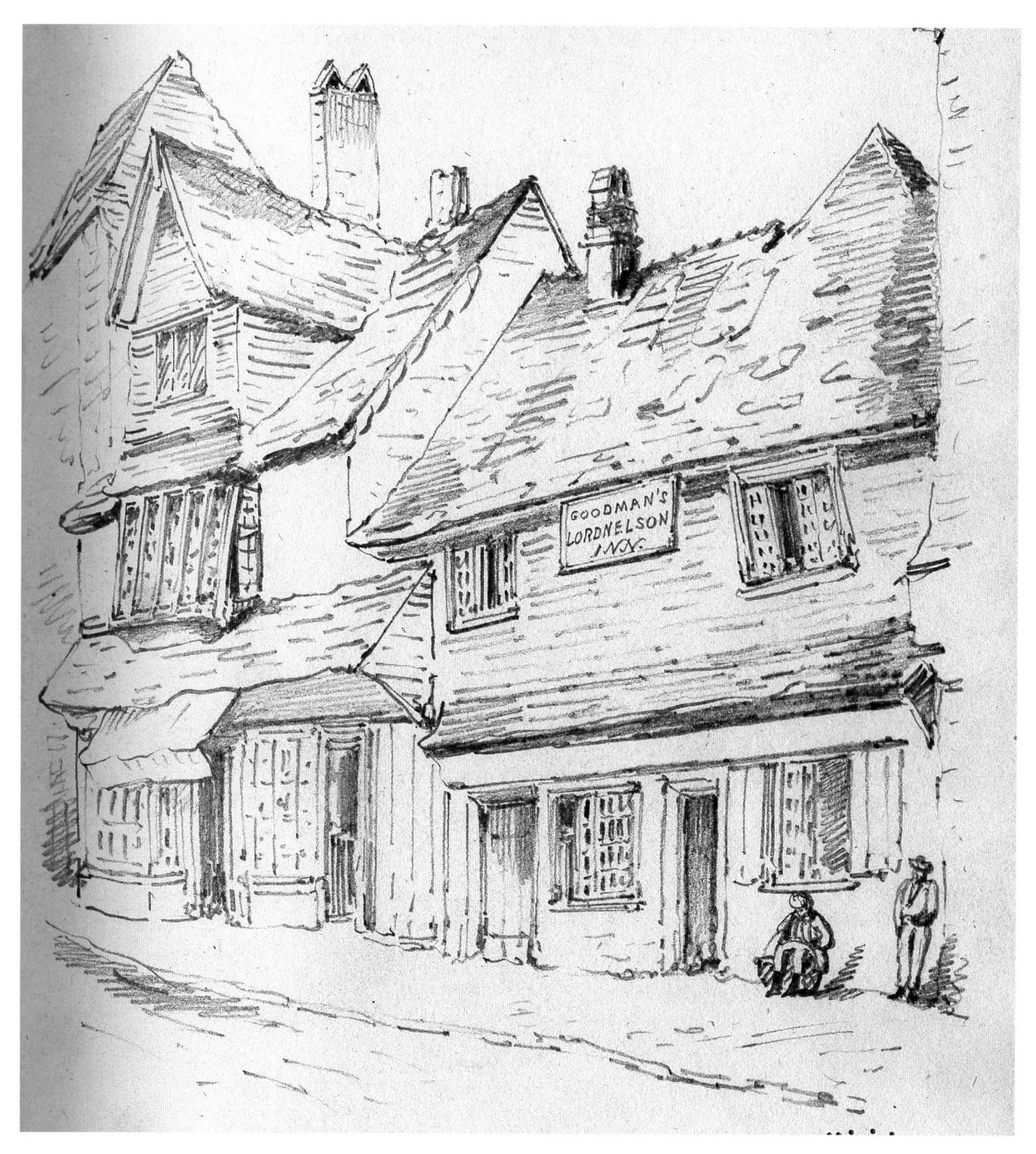

53. Pencil drawing by N. W. Deckamant entitled 'Lord Nelson Inn, Totnes', August 1856. The Lord Nelson Inn still survives, at the bottom of Fore Street.

54. First of three photographs of Fore Street, c.1900, a favourite view for photographers.

55–6. There are slight differences between these early photographs of Fore Street.

BUILDINGS

Totnes, July 25th, 1762.

William Short begs leave to acquaint Gentlemen, Ladies, and others that he hath opened that old Accustomed Inn, known by the sign of the Angel, or Gate House, in Totnes, in the County of Devon, where all gentlemen Travellers, and others who please to honor him with their company may depend on genteel accommodation and civil usage, and their favours will be gratefully acknowledged by their most obedient humble servant.

N.B. The old Angel is repaired and furnished in a very neat manner, and consists of four parlours, a large dinning room that runs quite across the street, fifteen lodging rooms, two kitchens, a coach-house, and convenient stabling for upwards of forty horses, three parlours and light lodging rooms are hung with genteel and fashionable paper. Mr James Willis at The Prince Eugene Inn has left off trade.

The arch was once divided into two, a narrow passage for pedestrians and a wider one for traffic.

The Arch has been altered and amended by removing the small archway and the large butment between, throwing it into the main archway and turns a capital Gothic Arch over the whole. The job was done by Webber the Builder and finished just about June 10 1837. My birthday.

The Diary of John Chaster, 1836–1841

57. Undated drawing by Hannaford. The dating of both images is interesting. A suggested date of the first for 1850 is clearly wrong given the clock was not installed until 1878. But neither is accurate, as South Street has been eliminated from the scene. They are both probably twentieth-century flights of fancy. In more troubled times the town gates were closed at night. For many years, it seems, the gatehouse and arch were used as an inn.

BUILDINGS

58. Undated line drawing by W. Brown. In 1850 Lord Seymour purchased the Gatehouse and opened it to the public as a Mechanics' Institute and Reading Room. The clock and turret were added between 1878 and 1880, financed by public subscription. The structure we see today looks ancient but is of course a recent reconstruction following the disastrous fire of 4th September 1990. The four-storey building on the left – 70 Fore Street – is Totnes Museum, a grade one listed building and supreme example of a late sixteenth-century merchant's shop and house.

59. Pencil drawing by N. W. Deckamant, August 1856, entitled 'Fore Street, Totnes'. A view before the clock and tower were added in 1878.

BUILDINGS

60. Pencil drawing by N. W. Deckamant, August 1856, entitled 'in Fore Street, Totness'. By 1857 there was a straw bonnet maker named Susan Briggs, this may be her shop. Note the advertisement for an excursion train to Torquay.

61. Pencil drawing by N. W. Deckamant, August 1856, entitled 'Fore Street, Totnes'. A view down High Street from a viewpoint next to Nicholas Ball's house (Number 16, now Barclay's Bank). To the left can be seen the pillars of Church Walk which eventually were used to support the roof of the Guildhall. The large house first on the left was the Church House which in the sixteenth century was owned by the Ball family. Four houses along (Number 7) was the Police Station in 1881.

BUILDINGS

62. Pencil drawing by N. W. Deckamant entitled 'Guildhall steps, Totnes', August 1856. Now known as Ramparts Walk which is accessed just under the arch in High Street.

TOTNES

63. Undated coloured drawing. These are the 'Middle' almshouses that John Hannaford pulled down. They once occupied the north side of the High Street, from the East Gate up to the church house. Fragments of the stone window frames are on display in the museum.

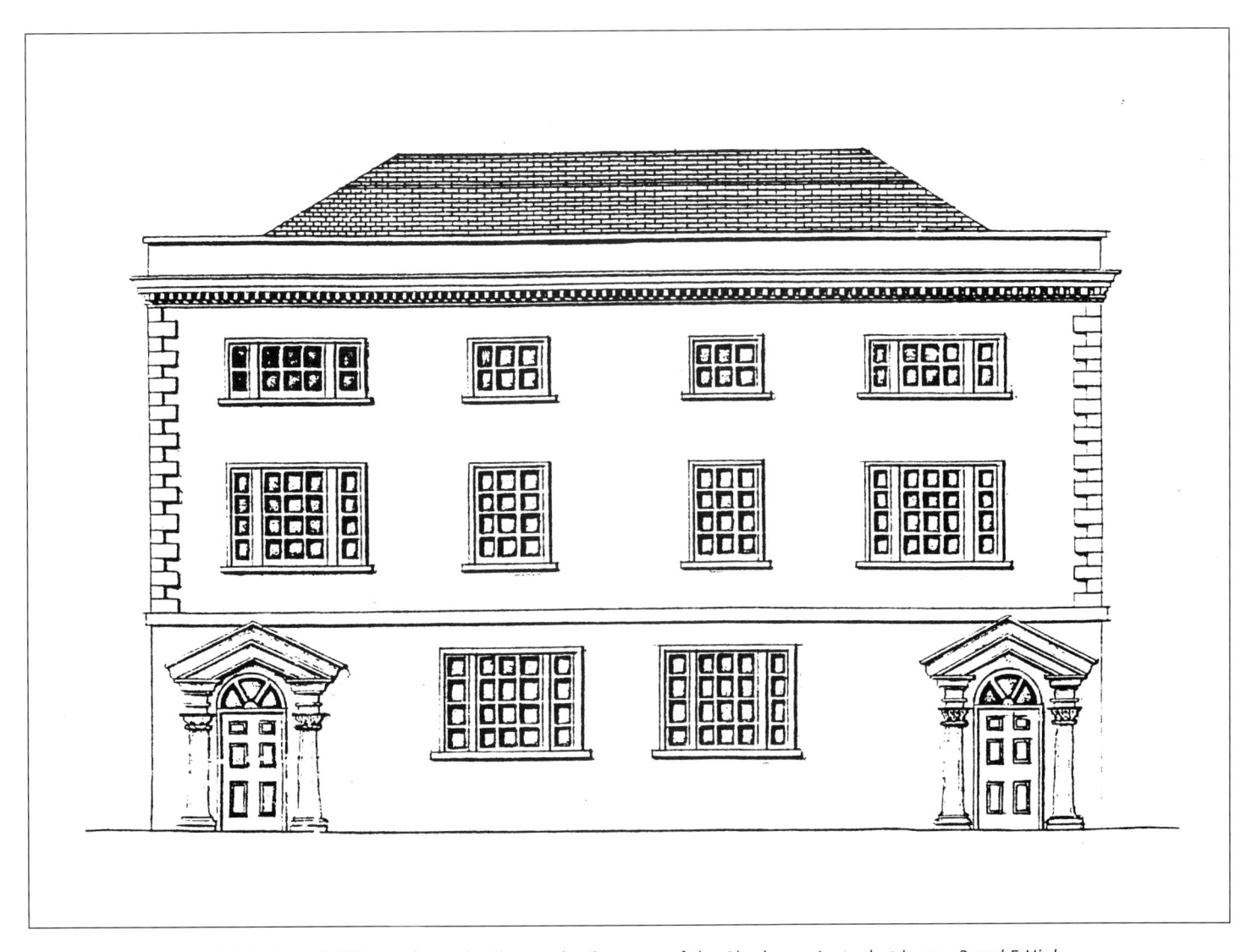

64. This design of 1782 was for a plot 'known by the name of the Almshouses', at what is now 3 and 5 High Street. It is attached to an indenture between Totnes Corporation and builder John Hannaford. Hannaford was 'at his own cost to pull down the Almshouses'. The design did not allow for the gradient of the High Street, and two houses were eventually erected to a different design on two levels, but the doorways are still similar to those shown here.

TOTNES

65. Undated photograph of the Guildhall. Ramparts Walk follows the curve of the old town wall. A Benedictine priory was established here in 1088, ultimately expropriated and demolished by order of Henry VIII. It was a ruin in 1540, but in 1553 the young King Edward VI gave permission for a new Guildhall, prison and grammar school to be built upon its foundations. The date can be seen on an inscription inside the Guildhall on the east wall. Within a week King Edward was dead at the age of 16, and it is probable that Totnes was the last of the many grammar schools he established. The school can be seen in the background of William Spreat's print of St Mary's church (see page 80). In 1886 the school was relocated in the Mansion in Fore Street, and this building was converted for use as a police station. Today it houses the Totnes Town Council offices, with a flat above. The old stone lintels were reused in the modernization and can be seen above the windows, and the original 'arrow slits' in the remains of the walls of the priory vaults are visible at the rear of the building.

66. Pencil drawing by N. W. Deckamant, August 1856, entitled 'Guildhall, Totnes'. Many changes have taken place. In 1878 when the pillars were removed from outside the church, the wall behind the gentleman depicted was demolished, the roof extended and the pillars (dated 1617) were installed for support. The wall which was demolished was part of the prison building. The gateway to the left leads into the churchyard.

67. View of the Guildhall by R. Granger Barrett entitled 'The Old Guildhall, Totnes', undated.

BUILDINGS

68. A painting of the Guildhall, c.1900.

TOTNES

69. Coloured wash by R. H. Froude entitled 'At the back of Mr Tom's house, Totnes, August 3 1795'. An examination of the Elbow Room in North Street will show how little this view has changed.

BUILDINGS

70. Pencil drawing by N. W. Deckamant entitled 'Church Lane and Lower Totnes', 1856, perhaps one of the most interesting drawings in the book. This shows the houses that backed onto the west side of the church, now demolished. There does not seem to be any other record of these buildings. The houses must have been extremely small and cramped and built almost on top of the church. In the distance the Priory Gates can be seen.

71–2. Two views of the North Gate, the first a copper line engraving by S. Rawle, 1810 and the second a lithograph by and after William Spreat, c.1845. The North Gate is situated below the Castle on the east side. Spreat's print, as ever, looks millimeter accurate, whereas Rawle gives an impression of the scene which omits the steep incline.

BUILDINGS

TOTNES

73. Pencil drawing by N. W. Deckamant entitled 'arch in Castle Street, Totnes', August 1856.

74. View of the North Gate by Edna Arthur, 1948.

75. *This undated view is of the reverse side of the North Gate.*

BUILDINGS

76–7. Two pencil drawings by N. W. Deckamant entitled 'Castle Street, Totnes', August 1856, looking up towards the Castle Inn with the North Gate behind. All these buildings remain although some additional building has taken place infilling the gaps between the houses.

TOTNES

BUILDINGS

78. View by Edna Arthur. At the end of Castle Street, and a short way along Fore Street lies the Narrows. This mid twentieth-century sketch is drawn looking back from the location of the now lost West Gate.

79. Pencil drawing by N. W. Deckamant, August 1856, entitled 'Fore Street Totnes'. A beautiful drawing of the Butter Walk which is largely unchanged today. The small shop on the left on the corner of Castle Street was originally the fish market but has since been demolished and replaced by a larger building now used as a bank. The covered walkways were used in the past to give shelter to stall holders on market day.

BUILDINGS

80. Coloured wash by R. H. Froude, 1825, entitled 'At the back of the Shambles, Totnes'. This can be seen by following the southern boundary of the old town along South Street, until the road divides into an upper and lower level. This scene has changed considerably since Froude's view. The Shambles – the flesh Shambles – was a meat market dating back at least to 1606, and it stood at what is now the car park at the rear of the Civic Hall. There was a Shambles Gate Inn here in 1823, indicating the existence of a Shambles Gate which, it has been suggested, was the town south gate, giving a satisfyingly complete set for the four principal compass points.

The Church of St Mary

St Mary's Church was built or perhaps re-built in the fifteenth century (around 1432 in the reign of Henry VI). The church is built of red stone with white Beer stone facings.

81. Copper line engraving by J. Greig after S. Prout, 1811. The artist could not have stood at this distance away from the church in 1850. Until 1878 the church was practically hidden from view of the High St by a two-storied building known as the Church Walk. This was an open granite arcade erected by Richard Lee in the seventeenth century and formed the frontage of this building. The boundary next to the churchyard was a solid wall with a gateway about eight feet wide that being the only space through which the south side of the church could be seen. There is a good view of the houses on the left, which were built very close to the west door. A visit to the churchyard will prove how very small these houses must have been.

THE CHURCH OF ST MARY

82. Drawing by Edna Arthur, mid twentieth-century, of the main entrance to the church of St Mary.

83–4. Two lithographs by and after William Spreat, 1842 and c.1850. These two views of the church of St Mary could easily have been made at the same time with an interval of perhaps several minutes to allow for the man contemplating the grave on the left hand side of the picture to move to the right hand side to speak to a woman also visiting the churchyard or perhaps he was asking the way to the grave in which case the order of the drawings would be reversed. The engravings have been made before the renovations of 1867, commenced, under the auspices of Gilbert Scott. According to contemporary reports the church was in a poor state of repair at this time. It can be seen from the engravings that the belfry windows having lost their mullions and tracery were filled with plain wooden louvres the full width of the openings. The churchyard is rather unkempt and the graves have a neglected air. The East window of the chancel has been entirely removed and the window opening has been filled in to facilitate the installation of an Italianate plaster baldicchino as an altar-piece. At the north East corner of the building an archway exists running diagonally through the two buttresses. These buttresses indicate that other buildings formerly abutted on this angle of the church. To the left of the picture can be seen houses which backed onto the churchyard in Church Lane and to the right is the Guildhall and the building which housed the Grammar School. The front porch of the church has wooden doors in front of the original door to the church. There is a dormer window in the roof thought to have been installed to introduce more light when extra seating was created in the gallery of the church in the eighteenth century.

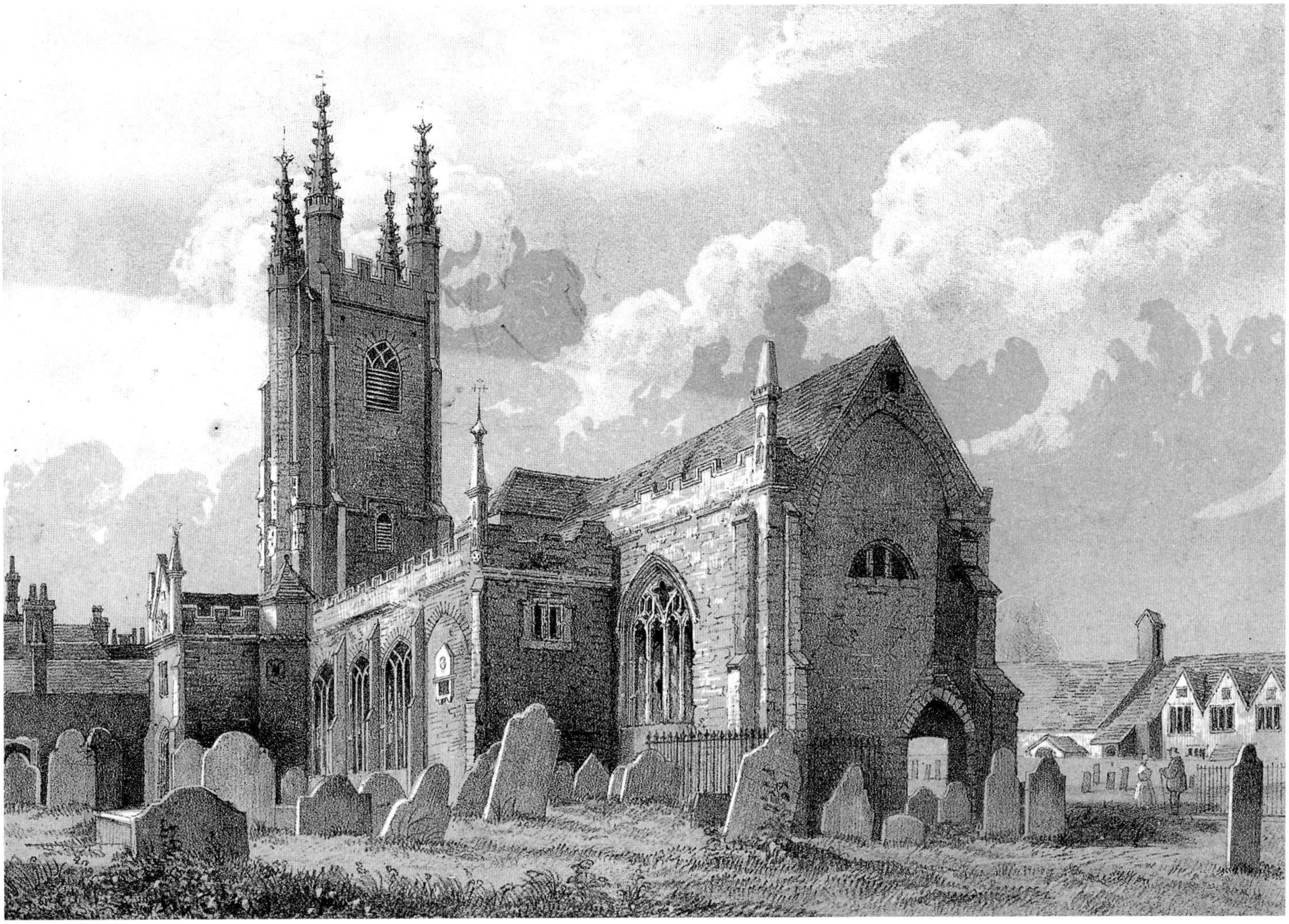

85. Steel line engraving by H. Wallis after W. H. Barlett, 1831. This picture tells a different story. The drawing was executed at an earlier time and one feels the jollity and gaiety of the people out for a stroll possibly on a Sunday. The reverence of the previous pictures is missing. Washing is fluttering in the breeze, and the gravestones are being used as seats. There are far fewer gravestones than in the previous drawings indicating that marking graves with headstones was a rather late convention. It is thought that the east window was filled in about 1799 to accommodate the altarpiece. Note the more explicit drawing of the houses in Church Walk and a different style of building depicted where the Grammar school was.

86. Undated photograph of the east end of the church.

TOTNES

87–8. *Two views of the interior of the church. The first is a copper line engraving by F. Nash after Samuel Lysons, 1822, and the second is a line engraving by and after Llewellynn Jewitt, 1850. These two pictures are separated in time by about 40 years. The carved stone screen is arguably one of the most interesting features of the church. In these two pictures the screen in all its intricacies is beautifully and accurately drawn. Little of the history of the screen is known. In an eighteenth century lawsuit a quotation from a book now lost states '38 Henry VI (1459–60) this year was an order made that the chancel shall be divided from the church with freestone as the cathedral church of Exon was'. Where the freestone came from is not recorded.*

The ancient rood gallery some nine feet in from east to west extending over the chancel and chapel screens was filled with pews facing westward. The approach to the rood loft on the right of the engravings was by the narrow stone staircase on the north side of the chancel eastward of the arch opening into the chapel. This staircase remains today but has now been blocked off. The loft extended originally across the north and south chapel. By 1860 the whole of the area above south chapel had been converted into a vestry and most of the south loft had been destroyed in the process. Looking at the two engravings some differences are very evident.

The engraving in Lysons' history of the county published in 1822 shows the ceiling beneath the loft formed into panels by moulded ribs with carved bosses at the intersections the outer cornice being enriched with foliage but the engraving from Cotton's history published in 1850 and executed by Jewett shows the ceiling with a few small ribs forming plain panels and without enrichments on the cornice. Lysons shows on the side of the passage leading from the staircase to the loft what appear to be paintings of the arms of four bishops and the arms in each case impaled with those of the see and on the left hand side of the engraving, as a protection, there is a fence of turned balusters. Both these features are missing from Jewitt's picture. Charles R. Baker King reported that this was how he found the interior in 1860. The pews were of painted deal.

89. *A detailed lithograph of the interior of the church by William Spreat about 1850 and before the restoration began. A contemporary description of the interior of the church before Sir Gilbert Scott's restoration commenced states 'what chiefly struck the eye of the visitor on entering the church apart from the beautiful screen was the extent and arrangement of the galleries'. Galleries were built on the west side and extended out as far as the middle pillar. The pews were in tiers one above the other similar to a theatre. The rood loft that can be seen running the width of the church was filled with pews looking westward. The north aisle had also had a gallery fitted with plain benches not pews. The galleries had covered so much wall space that the pillars had been made use of to receive monuments and tablets.*

If we look closely at the engraving by Speat we can see a memorial tablet hung on one of the pillars. Three others are on the wall to the right of the picture. In 1630 Thomas Westcote in his View of Devonshire recorded over sixty memorial tablets most of which are annotated in John Prince's Worthies of Devon.

The corporation seats in front of the screen either side of the chapel and chancel doors, are plainly visible. Resting on these are carved oak columns supporting a cornice extending across the central aisle carrying the Royal and the Town arms with the date 1636. As can be seen the ground floor of the church was crowded with pews these were made of deal and highly painted. These pews were of such restricted width that kneeling was impossible and the seat boards in each pew were placed opposite each other on three sides so that their occupants faced each other and many sat with their backs towards the chancel and pulpit.

On the left of the picture stands the pulpit over which hangs a sounding board and canopy of wood surmounted by a gilt angel. The pulpit in this picture was of stone and painted to imitate oak and was ornamented with gothic panelling and shields of modern emblazonment with devices of the tribes of Israel and Judah on it. The brass chandelier was donated to the church in 1760 and remains in this position today. The floor of the church was paved at this time and the many memorial stones were removed when tiles were laid during the restoration.

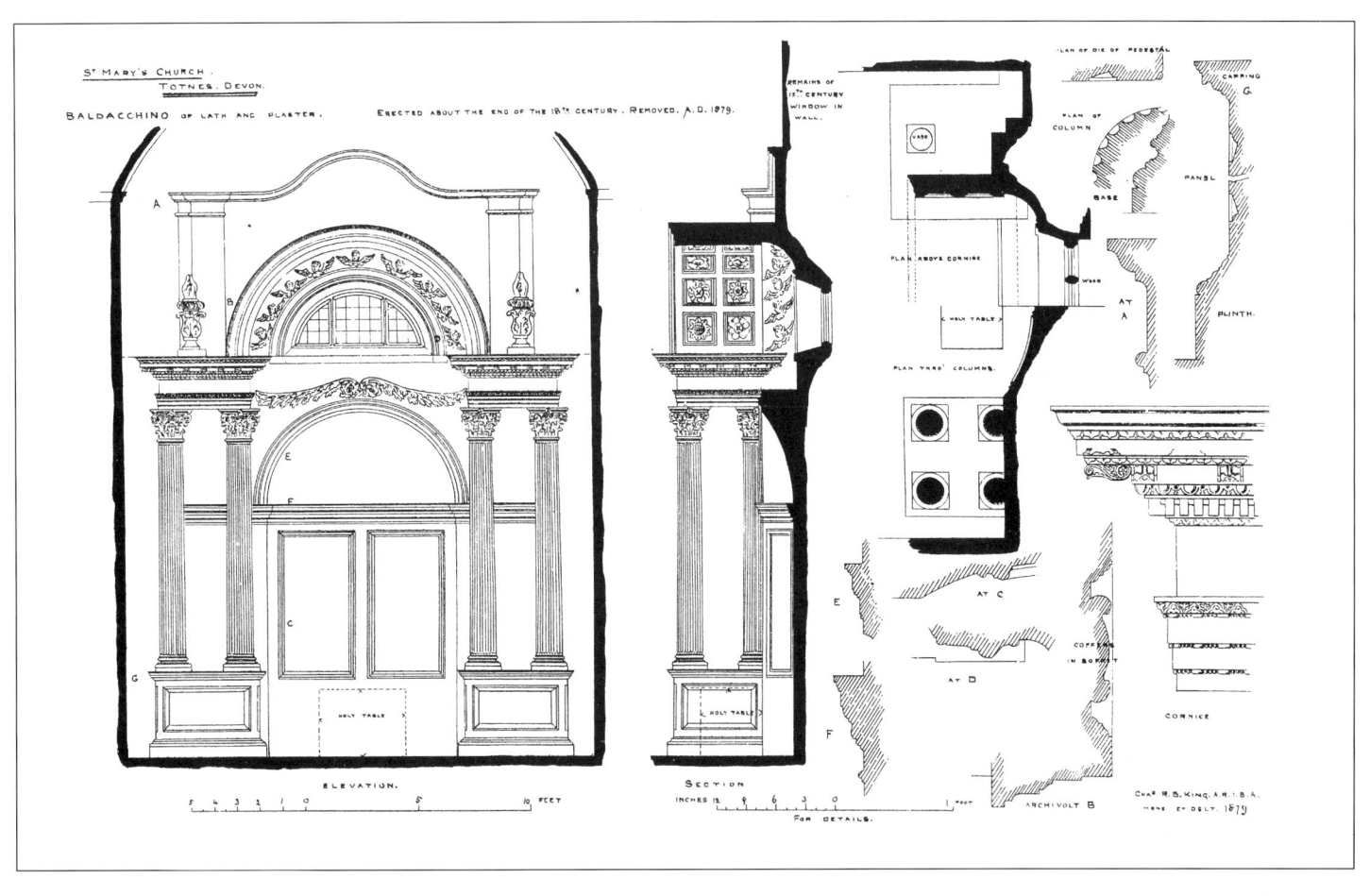

90. Plan by Charles R. B. King, 1879, of the Baldacchino. A lithograph by Charles King A.R.I.B.A, dated 1879. The baldacchino, more commonly spelled baldachin or baldaquin, is a structure in the form of a canopy. The altarpiece, occupied the whole height and width of the eastern end of the chancel and replaced the east window which was removed and the opening filled in with stone. It was made of white plaster and was of good classic design. Four Corinthian columns on each side supported an arched top or canopy beyond which was a shallow curved recess in which stood the Holy table. The date of this altarpiece was unknown but it was thought to have been erected about 1799. Because of the rarity of baldacchino in England and the excellence of the design Sir Gilbert Scott's architect Charles King attempted to dismantle it in sections to be erected elsewhere as an interesting relic. However the timberwork of which the framework was constructed proved to be so fragile that it was impossible to save it. Charles King made this lithograph and this is all we have to inform us of what the altarpiece looked like. This is a most unlikely object to find in a Devon church. In 1850 William Cotton in his Sketch of Totnes *stated that it is 'a most inappropriate and misplaced Corinthian altar piece' and continues 'it is truly lamentable to see so many of our parochial churches disfigured by the introduction of such incongruities'. The altar piece had been donated to the church by a resident of Totnes who must remain anonymous as no record has been found either of the date of installation or the donor.*

The Castle

The Castle was built by Judhael in the eleventh century using local labour on a man made mound outside the town wall. In the Domesday Book we are told that because it was constructed outside the wall no houses had to be demolished in Totnes. Unlike Barnstaple which lost 23 dwellings out of 59 and Lydford which lost 40 out of 68.

Throughout the 950 years that the Castle has stood overlooking Totnes it has had many owners and as far as is known has never been used in a defensive role. The manorial court was held there in the twelfth and thirteenth centuries. In 1530 Leland describes it as a ruin. In 1647 Lord Goring used it as his headquarters and 3 men were hanged there that year. Today the Castle is owned and maintained by English Heritage and receives many visitors each year.

91. Line engraving of the town seal, 1850. The earliest known impression of The Great Seal of the Mayor and Community of the Burg of Totnes is upon a deed of 1387 when John Russell was Mayor. It is not certain in which year the Seal was first adopted. The device is of a water gatehouse flanked by two towers, a central and higher tower surmounting the gate and a large key on either side. This may indicate the pride of the burgesses in the importance of the town as a Royal fortress. In Elizabethan times the borough arms were recorded as a similar device. After some indecision as to whether the gate should stand above water or not it was decided to have 'a water barry wavy' as a base. The motto 'the keys of knowledge will open any gate' was adopted.

92. Line engraving by and after Jewitt, 1850. A pastoral view of the Castle which belies the encroachment of the Caste ditch by housing gardens and a toffee factory. Trees grow on the Castle mound and ivy covers the gateway. A visitor walks laboriously to the top and an elderly lady is out for a stroll. At the date of this engraving it would have been an amenity for the whole town to enjoy as the Castle and grounds had been recently given by the Duke of Somerset for recreational use.

THE CASTLE

93. Pencil drawing by N. W. Deckamant entitled 'entrance to keep, Totnes Castle', August 1856. The entrance to the keep in Totnes Castle. For many years the Castle was shrouded in ivy and trees grew inside the keep and on the castle mound. Some of the neglect of this time can be seen from the small tree growing out of the wall in this drawing.

94. Lithograph by and after William Spreat, c.1850, of the priory and priory lands. This pastoral scene is sadly no more. All the fields shown in this etching were priory lands and consisted of gardens and orchards. All have been built upon. To the left is the Guildhall with the church beyond, to the right is the castle partially occluded by foliage of the trees on the mount. The house in the far right of the picture is referred to by William Cotton in 1850 as 'the dwelling house adjoining the Ashburton Road which still preserves the name of the Priory'. This house still exists and has recently undergone extensive restoration. The priory was dedicated to St Mary and was endowed in the reign of William the Conqueror by Judhael. The original site of the priory is thought to have been close to the present church and Guildhall.

95. This splendid if somewhat eccentric drawing presents a puzzle. The artist is unknown as is the date and the location of the artist when it was drawn. It is impossible today to obtain a view of the Castle as it is in the picture with the church on the right. However, it is possible that it was drawn as a composite picture to illustrate the narrative and that the church and houses were included just as an indication that the town in the following poem was Totnes.

On close inspection the picture is intriguing. Along the bottom of the drawing is a wall with two gates let into it. A man (is that a gun in his hand?) is leaning on the left hand gate. What is he aiming at? Close scrutiny reveals a bird flying above the hedgerow near the first house on the left. A seagull perhaps? Moving along to the right from the man with the gun we come to a rider with his horse at full gallop. We are told in the narrative that 'he has come from afar and is in haste to meet his child'. As on all Devon roads to this day there is a slow moving farm vehicle in front of him to impede his progress. Above the road the Castle mound has been terraced and used as gardens and orchards. On one of the terraces a woman is hanging out washing and a man standing to her right is pointing to the road and the rider beneath. Is this the mother of the child and the wife of the horseman? On the battlements the child with her companions is waving to the rider. There is a flag fluttering in the breeze. Which flag is it?

In general the castle appears in a state of disrepair and neglect. Ivy covers the battlements and trees grow in the stone fabric of the building. This terracing of the mound was recently the cause of a land slip and reconstruction work had to be implemented to prevent the earth from the mound demolishing the houses in Castle Court beneath. The seagull population appears to be as large it is in the present day. Above the drawing is written 'This picture represents a beloved little girl on its summit waving her handkerchief and supported by her guardian. The parent in the foreground is from afar and in haste to meet his child.' Underneath the drawing is the following poem:

THE CASTLE

What? this old castle still remains
Yes! What deeds of did they bespeak
Here heroes fought with crimson Gore
No thoughts of death to end their fate
Sir Walter Rally (sic) here is famed
When Totnes was a seaport town
Tobacco and potatoes a foreign produce was
He sought and brought to our Land.
The cruel times in which he lived
To London Tower an exile he was sent
'Tis there the Blood Axe ends his fate
Pomeroy too may here be traced
With men and steed of ancient race

Their possessions lost the Blood Axe to escape
For cruel were the days in which they lived
They and their blindfolded steed were madly hurled
To death thrown down the aweful precipice.
Since here---young men and maidens oft times meet
To build their Castles in the Air
Then let this old Castle still remain
Memento for old ancient Fame.

As far as it is known no battles were ever fought at the castle and it has never fulfilled a defensive function.

TOTNES

Country Houses

Three country houses, in and around the area, were of some particular importance to Totnes.

96. Anonymous aquatint of Follaton House, the home of the Cary family, 1827. The house was rebuilt for the Cary family in 1826 and used as a hospital during the first world war. In 1928 it was sold to the Cooperative Holidays Association and in 1965 purchased by Totnes Rural District Council. It is now the headquarters of South Hams District Council.

COUNTRY HOUSES

97. Another view of Follaton, a steel line engraving of 1830.

98. Copper line engraving by and after S. & N. Buck, 1734, of Berry Pomeroy Castle, Devon's most well-known ruins for several hundred years. This medieval castle was purchased by the Seymour family in 1547 at which time a programme of renovation began but it was left unfinished on the death of Edward, Duke of Somerset, five years later. The castle was not properly occupied for generations and lay in ruins by the end of the eighteenth century. It is now managed by English Heritage.

COUNTRY HOUSES

99. Lithograph of the castle, c.1848.

101. View of Sharpham, entitled 'Sharpham, the residence of Capt. Bastard R. N., M. P., from the property of his grace the Duke of Somerset', 1820. The house was rebuilt for Captain Philemon Pownall with privateering money and later passed to the Bastard and Durant families.

COUNTRY HOUSES

101. Steel line engraving of Sharpham, c.1850, by and after W. Spreat.

Select Bibliography

Bridget Cherry and Nikolaus Pevsner, *The Buildings of England: Devon* (1987)

William Cotton, *A Graphic and Historical Sketch of the Antiquities of Totnes* (1850)

Todd Gray, *Devon Country Houses and Gardens Engraved* (Exeter, 2001), I

Todd Gray, *Victorian News from Totnes* (Exeter, 2001)

C. R. Baker King, 'St Mary's Church', *Transactions of the Devonshire Association*, vol. 36, 1904

John Leland, The Itinerary, edited by R. Pearse Chope, *Early Tours in Devon & Cornwall*, Devon & Cornwall Notes & Queries, 1918

Bob Mann, *The Lost Folly of Totnes; Mayor Taunton and his Monument* (Totnes, 1999)

Bob Mann, *An Outline of Totnes History* (Totnes, 2002)

Percy Russell, *The Good Town of Totnes* (Exeter, 1963)

Hugh Watkin, *The History of Totnes Priory and Medieval Town* (Torquay, 1914–1917), two volumes

The Diary of John Chaster, 1836 – 1841

Exeter Flying Post

Monthly Magazine, 1808

Illustration Sources

Totnes Museum: 2, TM T516 (SC3400); 3, TM 55x/p6; 4, TM 74/15/14; 11 TM63/36w; 12, TM 63/37w; 13, TM 63/50w (SC3408); 19, 74/15/13; 27, TM 74/15/20; 31, T8 63/29W; 33, no reference number; 34, TM 65/8; 35, 1965.070; 39, 1967.032; 40, 2002.356 (SC3404); 42, no reference number; 44, TMT689; 45, 1963.031; 47–8, no reference number; 50, TM 50/1(X)A; 51, 1967.018; 58, 1963.042; 63, 2002.354; 67, 2002.326; 72, 1959.007; 73, TM 74/15/6; 76, 66/1P; 78, TM 65/8C; 78, 1966.001; 90, C. R. Baker, 'St Mary's Church', *Transactions of the Devonshire Association*, vol 36, 1904; 95, TM 83X/3.

Westcountry Studies Library: Introduction 1–4, A. W. Searle, *Totnes* and E/B/590; 1, SC3402; 5, SC3390; 6, SC3345; 7, SC3406; 8, SC3403; 9, SC3392; 10, PD8990; 14, SC3396; 15, SC20; 16, SC3394; 17, PD08243; 18, SC3391; 20, PD3040; 21, SC3388; 22, PD9003; 23, PD9917; 24, PD9918; 25, PD9916; 26, SC3397; 28, PD8955; 29, PD8946; 30, A. W. Searle, *Totnes*; 32, PD9000; 37, PD8958; 38, PD8961; 41, PD8913; 43, SC3370; 46, PD8952; 49, SC3372; 52, PD8945; 54, PD5337; 55 PD41910; 56, PD5472; 57, PD41911; 65, MPh E/B/595; 66, PD42788; 67, PD8930; 69, SC3386; 70, SC3387; 77, PD8956; 80, SC3380; 81, SC3378; 85, SC3377; 86, PD3066; 87, SC3376; 88, PD8504; 89, SC3379; 91–2 PD03061; 94, SC3401; 96, SC3383; 97, SC3384; 98, SC114; 99, SC 150; 100, SC17; 101, SC25.

Devon Record Office: 48, 5324Z/Z1; 36, 53, 59–60, 62, 64, 66, 68, 71, 74–5, 79, 93, Z19/31/2; 61